Hansel & Gretel

Get the Word on the Street

Al Ortolani

Rattle | *Studio City, California* | 2019

ISBN: 978-1-931307-42-0

First edition

Rattle Foundation
12411 Ventura Blvd
Studio City, CA 91604
www.rattle.com

CONTENTS

ACKNOWLEDGMENTS

Aethlon: The Journal of Sport Literature: "Game Prayer"
Algebra of Owls: "Teaching Hawthorne to High School Juniors"
Amaryllis: "Girls' Choir"
Camroc Press Review: "The Fifteen Dollar Vacation"
Clementine Unbound: "Shopping for Fruit"
Coal City Review: "A Lesson About the Bonks"
The Dead Mule School of Southern Poetry: "Hansel and Gretel Get the Word on the Street"
Failed Haiku: "First Seed"
The Galway Review: "Forgetting Dante in Third Period"
Great Weather for Media: "Daddy's Car"
Gutter Eloquence: "Biology Lab"
I-70 Review: "Continental Drift"
Lummox: "Corpse Pose"
Modern Haiku: "Frozen"
New Letters: "Seventh Grade Communication Arts"
Sonic Boom: "Passing Period"
Star 82 Review: "Key Card Dawn"
Tar River Poetry: "The Class That Would Not Eat," "Outside the English Department I Lock My Keys in My Car and Realize I Have No Inclination to Be Anywhere"
Victorian Violet Press and Journal: "At-Risk in Bonehead English"
Wild Goose Poetry Review: "Taking the ACT in December"
Wild Quarterly: "Syllabus Change in Late May"
Zeitgeist: "Pick-Up"

Some of the poems in this book, sometimes in different versions, were used in the following collections: *Finding the Edge* (Woodley Press); *Waving Mustard in Surrender* (NYQ Books); *Paper Birds Don't Fly* (NYQ Books); *On the Chicopee Spur* (NYQ Books).

"Hansel and Gretel Get the Word on the Street" was selected as a poem of the day in Jason Ryberg's *Head Full of Boogeymen/Belly Full of Snakes (or Confessions of a Low Status American Male)*, November 25, 2011.

Hansel & Gretel

Get the Word on the Street

Hansel and Gretel
Get the Word on the Street

You have tried leaving
a trail of bread crumbs
that will take you
back home to father,
but the grackles
eat them as soon
as your little sister
quits shooing them away.

The rest of the story
is scarier. There's
a witch at the edge of town
who will lock
precocious children
in a rabbit hutch.

She plans
to eat you, once
you're fattened up. After
which, the plot turns
confusing. I've
blocked it out

on account of the
violence, but I know
that you are pressured
to eat fast food: French
fries, hamburgers, chocolate
shakes. You're
required to stick
a bone, rather than
your finger through
the chicken wire.

[...]

Of course, only a moron
would confuse
a chicken bone for a finger,
but the word on the street
says you fake
your weight-gain. Eventually,
you'll catch the witch
off-guard. Then,
you slip out of the hutch,
push her in a pot
of boiling canola, and
get this, you eat her
candy house.

The witch, they say,
is mostly blind, probably
in the late stages of
macular degeneration. She has
lost her glasses,
and that's another part of
the story that I just
can't digest. The old
lady is shrewd.
She has chewed up little
boys and girls for years.
I mean WTF,
she works chat rooms.

She deploys multiple
user-names like Sweet Thing,
Tootsie Roll and Honey Buns.

Seventh Grade Communication Arts

For 50 cents the girl throws
herself across the hallway
and slams her head into the bathroom door.
She uses the money to buy candy
at the 7-Eleven across from school.
She shows up in my fifth hour with a bag
of red licorice, wax lips and a welt
on her forehead. She has
a twitch in her eye. No cellphone.
I tap her action verb worksheet.
She slides the sack in her backpack. Later,
I notice the red licorice in her lap.
She's nibbling like a rabbit.
I remind her to put up the candy.
The next time I look
she's wearing the wax lips.
I reach out my hand and she drops the lips
in my palm. I toss them in the trash.
Hey, she complains. How can I smile
if you trash my lips?

Eighth Grade Industrial Arts

Shop class frightened him,
the jigsaw, the planer, the lathe,
most of all the teacher
and his long, double-strapped paddle
that hung by the tool room door.
He was frightened by the raw oak
that he dreamed would become a bookshelf
where he'd rest his favorite copies
of *Robin Hood* and *Tom Swift*.
Unlike Eric or Wayne, he couldn't see
how to turn lumber into the photograph, p. 87,
in the shop text. From here to there
was lost to him, not unlike Latin
or basketball or junior high girls.
He feared everything in Shop Class,
the noise of the jigsaw, the vibration
of the blade, the proximity of his fingers
to the cut. He feared his stupidity,
his awkwardness with tools, the towering
man with the paddle, who appeared
to frown at his very existence, who took
his misshapen boards out of his hands,
and, in saving the boy from an F,
screwed them together
with thick, round-headed wood screws,
then, tossing it like a towel
onto the shop table, wiped his hands
clean on his navy apron.

Frozen

There is not a bird in the sky. A 9th grader walks the parking lot before school, his face a frozen fist. He shivers from the dead zero of the morning, hoodie pulled like a monk's cowl. He is earlier than the others, the building itself, still unopened. Without my key card, how long would he wait for the door? When he shuffles past into the hallway, he mumbles the frozen hello he saves for adults.

Grasshopper(inajarleaping)

Pick-Up

A rat in the grass outside the deli
picks through the salting of snow, flips
a leathery pepperoni with his claws
and wedges it into the slit of his mouth.

Two boys with a basketball,
heading home from the playground,
cross the drive-through to the curb.
The rat darts for the shelter of the sewer.

One boy heaves the basketball after him.
It skips on the pavement
and rebounds off a gas meter,
lodging like the shadow of a planet

between the gutter drain
and the snow-wet branches. The rat
rises, ball in his court.
The boys edge shoulder to shoulder

into the drift of sodden leaves.
They stoop with their hands
wedged in their hoodies:
ball within reach, weather

picking up, sleet in the face
beginning to sting.

A Lesson About the Bonks

One day while on lunch duty
the principal presses up to me
and says, now I've seen it all.
The two Bonk boys, absent all morning,
have just arrived in time
for their free or reduced lunch.
Watch them disappear before
the next bell rings. Mom and dad
are both sitting outside in the car.
It's a cycle the way families move
in this part of the county,
just ahead of the bill collectors. The Bonks
will be gone next month
and we won't see them again
until spring or fall. I can't blame the kids
for the dumbass parents who raise them,
but the cycle needs broken,
and you, young teacher,
with the fresh bachelor's degree
have got to snap it. Add some literacy.
Teach the Bonks to read.
You've got maybe two months.

At-Risk in Bonehead English

Sudden snow blew from the north
like a thin, crisp mistake, white and crystalline,
more powder than flake. Lacking in depth
of grace or beauty, it lay as an indignant
sheet of winter, a threat to the crocus
unfolding below the maple. Perhaps ice
turns me cold in the classroom, focused
on the boy who walks in without a pass
to visit the mouthy girl by the window,
the one whose name is scrawled on desks.
He chews gum, jaw muscles bursting under
pale, thin skin. His eyes dart across
the room, ready to challenge even winter.

Continental Drift

The freeze nearly killed mother's garden
after she took off with another man—cherry
tomatoes and marigolds remained.
Her three boys seldom talked at breakfast,
spooning cheerios, small buoys swelling
with milk, massing in a strange, drifting geography.
Dad explained that mom had gone south
with the robins and the finches and the IT guy
from the district office. If the house settled
or the floor furnace popped,
they flinched, opened sugary mouths like fledglings.
Lunches were packed the night before,
the day ahead discussed in metaphors of weather:
no snow expected, light rain by two,
chances of sleet by evening.
Dad set their book bags by the door.
They waited for the yellow bus they knew
from before the earth moved
to scrape the curb like the sun.

Biology Lab

The kids say she's
a bitch. The faculty
speaks of her as a tough nut.
The administration
highlights her students'
test scores. When parents
phone, she explains her goals
for teenagers with
a hopeful, optimistic
diplomacy. At night
she sifts through stacks

of lab reports, red ink
on her fingertips.
Early in her career
she thought
a perfect score might
change the world.
Tonight, she drinks
too much wine
and draws multi-colored
happy faces
on even
the weakest papers.
Rain loosens the last

leaves. Geese fly south
in football season. She
remembers them chattering
below the clouds like
cheerleaders.

Corpse Pose

Faculty meeting:
I lock my door, turn out the light, and
close my eyes on the floor.

           There was a colleague
who used to nap during her planning period.
She was old and tired. I kept an eye
on the clock for her, making sure that she
was up five minutes before the bell. She said
she needed to be "recomposed
              before she decomposed."

Students start to swarm the hallways;
one rattles my doorknob.
I wonder if my feet are visible, sticking out
from under my desk like a body under
a dumpster. Will the school nurse burst
into the room with the Resource Officer?
How do I explain this yoga corpse
during a faculty meeting?

           But no one comes,
and that in itself is a lonely thought.
I unlock the classroom door, high five
the first students through.

Ms. W Explains Roethke to AP English

Even if they'd seen a waltz, they'd never
danced one. Oh, they knew the word, like we might
know the words pan flute or bacchanalia. So, when I heard
Ms. W's fifth hour go dumb as wall paste,
the definition vague and untendered, I stepped
into the classroom and held out my arms.
She took my left hand, and I slipped my right
around her back (keeping safe distance);
we began to waltz the room. At first bumping
into desks, the trash can, a computer printer,
then finding space, built into a rhythm that allowed
the *123 123* to swing. The class laughed, as we laughed,
a moment of clowning turned graceful, one
they'd recall in posts and tweets.
But for Roethke, I said as we stopped,
and I brushed one student's desk free of books and papers,
his father had been drinking. He slammed
into the world with a belt buckle.
Ms. W stepped onto my shoes, and I would have
careened around the room, as if with my daughter,
except that I couldn't lift my feet. Give him
your sober countenance, she said, as we bent
and swayed in imitation, one that
cannot unfrown itself. Some got the point,
staring at their knuckles on the page.

Outside the English Department Lock My Keys in My Car and Realize Have No Inclination to Be Anywhere

Luckily, it is a bright November day
and the orange leaves outside the English
Department are falling like lazy sparrows.
The officer from campus security is a tall
blonde woman. She's never met
a door she couldn't unlock. I ask her
if she knows how to spell dumbass.
She grins, what's your name? She pries
the door open a quarter of an inch, jams it
with a plastic wedge. Then she begins
fishing into the cab with a long metal rod.
I can't recall but it's either pink or green
and bent and twisted from long use.
With the hook on the end she slowly
turns the window handle. She leans against
the vehicle, the reflection
of the orange leaves and the lazy sparrows
begins to sink into the frame of the door,
my Starbucks cooling in the cup holder.

Teaching Hawthorne to High School Juniors

The old trunk has casters.
A boy rolls it, squeaking
like a thousand bats,
down the hallway
so that he can turn its
flat top into a desk.
Sitting on the floor
to write is difficult
for some. The teacher
uses the change in venue
to engage students.
That's why she allows
the trunk, the boy,
the squeaking wheels,
to set her teeth
on edge, to give her
cold chills. Everyone
listens, unable to write
until the squeaking
stops. The minister's
black veil,
lifted only at death,
reveals a dead guy,
little more,
the village, the class
of 11th graders,
still bored.

The Class That Would Not Eat

Fourth hour goes bonehead in spring.
I'd say they're selectively bright.
Occasionally, I have to take
the host of knowledge
and lay it on their tongues,
and even then, on bad days, it just
falls out from between their teeth
onto the gray carpet. I swear
they are clumsy learners. History,
math, the sciences, are dribbled
across their school spirit-wear
like baby effluvia, Melba
toast crumbs, spittle. They explain
to me in their polite way that old
literature is too boring to swallow,
much less digest. They want the
The Outsiders or Harry Potter, both
of which were ladled out in 8th grade.
Fifty Shades of Gray, one girl laughs.
I offer them the Canterbury Tales,
a slice of Middle English on black
bread. This is something you
would not choose for yourselves.
The taste promotes menu literacy,
and that too makes no sense to them.
They regurgitate it as fast as I can
spoon it in. You are picky learners,
I say at last. No peas. No carrots.
Just chicken fingers, slavered in ketchup,
a Starbuck latte,
topped with whipped cream.

Forgetting Dante in Third Pe

I was reading Canto 34 to my senior English clas
Virgil was climbing out of circle nine; Dante
slugged toward Purgatory. The storm
that had been building in charcoal clouds
hit the windows—lightning shimmered, thunder l
All seven rows turned to watch.
Spines cracked—terza rima flattened. Twenty-seve
copies of the Ciardi translation
hit the wood.
It was a tremendous moment
for forgetting centuries of literature. The rain
streamed in sheets across the glass. One girl
claimed the whole world
was getting scrubbed in a carwash.

First Seed

My wrestling team lifted a Bible from a motel in 1975, the cover red with white lettering. School colors. At the State Regionals they broke a television, collapsed a bed, and picked fights at the 7-Eleven. Forty years later, the Gideon is still the first thing I unpack at the beginning of the school year. My desk is stuffed with talismans, a broken stop watch, a detention slip, a whistle. Even this beat-up Bible, lifted while they emptied their pockets to pay the damages—binding loose, pages yellowed. No one the wiser.

> iris in the rain
> thumbprint
> on your photograph

Game Prayer

Maybe it's the way boys
look at each other before the last game,
their eyes wet and glimmering with rain.

Maybe it's that I catch them
in these shy moments of waiting,
turning the world like a pigskin,

flipping it nonchalantly, low spiral
drilling the air. Maybe it's this
moment before the splash of lights

before the game prayer
before you run from the door.
If so, forgive me

for seeing you so vulnerable,
in that quiet moment
before the helmets.

Tough Cookies

smoke at the bowling alley
on Christmas night.
They bounce on their toes
below the *Open* sign
for warmth.
Swirls of snow brush
down Broadway, multi-colored
lights blinking in evergreens.
Two security employees
from the casino creep
into the bowling alley parking lot.
They drive a beat-up Bronco, windshield
encrusted with sleet—scraped
to two dark slits.
The chains on their tires
jingle across the ice.
The tough girls share
a tube of cherry lipstick.
They check their breath
by singing "O Holy Night"
into their hands.

Daddy's Car

Five a.m. in the cold—
a girl warms the Cherokee
before emptying the remaining
Xanax down her throat.
She doesn't want to fall
asleep shivering, ice crystals
up her nose. She wonders
if she has enough gas
to keep the motor
running. She depends
on the car, the reassuring
timing of the engine, the heater
on full, even a little
light from the dash.
It would ruin everything
if the car died, the engine
pinging as it cooled
to silent steel.

Key Card Dawn

Early morning geese pull the darkness behind them, tugging the fabric of night to the west. Their voices waggle above the rooftops, somewhere beyond my sight. They are shadows against a larger shadow. My truck motor pings as it cools, parking spot filled. Once more I hear the flock before I swipe my key card through the lock. I turn. Dawn is lifting, a slit of light, a curtain opening between the night sky and the sleeping city. Often, I am the first one in the building. It is a time for whispering furnaces and buzzing electric lights. There is no one to love except in generalities: students, colleagues, motivations for the good of mankind. There is a hard to reach itch in the center of my back. I square up to an edge in the hallway and grind the brick.

>   one street light caught
>   in patches of ice, guessing
>   shapes below snow

Space Walk

Iced by light mist, the high
school lot reflects the headlights
of the early arrivals—exhaust
snakes from tailpipes, rubber tires
crunch crusts of ice, Jupiter
high in the west, Venus low
in the south, both brilliant
with indifference like
Christmas lights to the blind.
The janitor ministers to thermostats
and salts the stairs as quietly
as a monk. The short bus
labors up the drive. Paraprofessionals
converge at the side door
and release the hydraulic lift.
The only student is rolled out,
chair balanced at the tip
of the steel edge. A boy, bundled
in a Bronco's parka, legs
wrapped in sweats, waits
to be lowered to the curb,
his Air Jordans bright
like planets.

Taking the ACT in December

High school seniors file in this morning
to take the ACT. They are taught the future
hinges upon a two-digit score that will
open doors. It's a cold morning,
the roads covered with ice. The proctor
carries a cup of Starbucks and a stack
of essays to grade. She is young, just
a year or two beyond college herself.
The boys tap their pencils, wondering
if she is the one who will
meet them after the test, after their scores
are compiled, after the doors open. The girls
study her more closely: her boots,
her tights, her layered hair, the way
she shuts off her phone
and drops it—finished into her bag.

The Fifteen Dollar Vacation

Two teachers on winter break access Netflix
and download all five seasons of *Breaking Bad*.
She makes popcorn and he brings in a 12 pack
from the garage. Somewhere in season two
he lights his father's calabash and stokes it
with the stash he found in the evergreen
across the street. They dim the lights and put the set
on mute. Like kids, they text secret messages
to each other, phones on vibrate. He wakes after
midnight to the wind—tree limbs tapping the siding,
sighing as snow runs the eaves, corners
the chimney. She is still sleeping, the blue throw
pulled up to her chin. The couch is narrow—
the remote control lost in the cushions.

Girls' Choir

A dark-haired girl sits in the center of the choir room pecking out songs on the piano. Her classmates are giggling through study hall. Some lounge on the floor texting, studying their phone screens. Another has isolated herself and connects dots in an AP English assignment. The girl at the piano returns to a fragment of a song which is reminiscent of McCartney's "Golden Slumbers." She plays around the melody. Maybe her song is something else, something more modern. Nevertheless, the energy in the room settles, girl linked to girl at 10 a.m.

    slits of sunlight
    through winter blinds, dancing
    blue fingernails

Drug Dog Visit

The police dog sniffs through
the building today. He barks
outside my classroom. The cop,
knowing my students, laughs
as they stiffen in their seats.
Soon they relax. Officer Smith's
just messing with us, they explain.
Well, it's a good thing
you left your grass at home, I joke.
The boys laugh again.
That isn't the half of it, one says.
(I don't want to know the half of it.)
So I say, let's get back
to your Kafka.
They lower their heads
and try to make sense of Gregor,
who, as a dung beetle, keeps himself
shyly tucked under a couch,
rather than terrifying the streets.
What's with this hiding, they ask.
A dung beetle could be
as cool as Ant Man. He could
hook up with the Wasp.

Switch Plate

The day moves by me, and I'm still
at the same old desk that was two-wheeled
into my room by the custodian. The lights
run on some kind of motion detector.
If no one moves, let's say, in ten minutes,
they blink out, and I have to raise my arms
and wave them like crazy. Possibly,
they click back on. Possibly, they don't.
At this point, I have to get up and walk
the room in the dark until the shadow of me
is recognized in the recesses of the switch
plate. Once in a while I'll have a class
of high school kids writing essays,
and the lights will suddenly black out,
and they will all look up astonished
like they've really done something cool.

Shopping for Fruit

What is melancholia? I ask
the class of 17-year-olds. One boy
just outside the T zone answers,
a fruit. And I had to laugh.
Yes, probably in the produce section
at HyVee, you've got the honeydew,
the cantaloupe, the melancholia,
most likely priced higher than
the watermelon, so germane to
family picnics, ice cream socials,
class reunions. The melancholia
ripens slowly on vines of discontent.
It is only purchased by the disillusioned
when the fruit bin has been emptied
of choices. But I keep this cherry
to myself. These boys haven't
done much produce shopping.
They still find bananas amusing.

Cream Cheese

Today, I found a poster
of a tombstone in my school mailbox.
It was rolled neatly like a scroll,
a well-positioned, blank tombstone
in dynamic color. I brought it back
to my classroom, wondering if
this was some type of guidance-related,
write-your-own epitaph project.
No explanation presented itself.
I taped the poster to my whiteboard
much to the dismay of my classes.
They couldn't understand who
would leave me such a gift,
which I suppose means that I am
a popular teacher, which in itself,
is an ambivalent title in a high school.
Who doesn't like to be liked? But
students are foremost survivalists,
an art form passed through generations.
They use Spark Notes, swell
font size, triple-space the double-spaced.
Seniors arrive mornings late for class
with bribes of Starbucks. I'm easily
suckered, stonewalled, amused.
If they include cream cheese,
they can write my epitaph with bagels.

At the State Soccer Tournament

Elementary school students
are playing near a sewer grate,
one girl with bright eyes
says, if we lift this up, meaning
the iron grate, we could get
inside. That's how it begins,
one idea out of the range
of the expected, and then there's
trouble. We could get inside,
she continues. And then what,
crawl through a pipe slicked
with sludge. Momentum
spirited the idea, but the others
just stood back and looked
at the wet hole at their feet.
The grate was firmly planted,
and would take a lot of digging
to lift. Their older brothers
on the soccer field have scored again,
a fluke shot that bounced
off the upper bar and into the net.
The other team, hanging their heads,
jogs back to center field,
where they begin again, passing
the ball wide for another drive.
The girl with the bright eyes,
and the command of an explorer,
has run off to the concessions
for a snow cone. She is too young
for the long haul, the lowering
of her blond locks over a shovel
and digging until her hands bleed.

Yellow Bees

I bring the second-grade baseball
team bubble gum, two bags of it.
I open the sacks and dump the pieces
into a single brown grocery sack.
I leave it on the dugout bench
and get out of the way, back to the
lawn chair under the single elm.
Moments later, when the first batter
comes up to the plate, I notice
his jaws, opening and closing
on the sweet pulp, chomping at the
plate before the whirring wheel
of the pitching machine. Each boy
is given five strikes before the coach
sets the T on the plate. Eventually,
when the bases are filled, Double
Bubble gum wrappers blow across
the infield with the dust and the
small yellow bees. No one loses
in second grade, not even Miller,
who, as a dyslexic, can't read,
stammers through the week,
but never needs the T. He can
drive a long shot 50 feet
over the shortstop's head.

Syllabus Change in Late May

Cracks of afternoon light slip through the blinds.
Finding Forrester plays on the DVD
while graduating seniors sneak

tweets on their smartphones. They cradle them
in their laps like fragile birds, dropping
bits of daydream into their open beaks.

The teacher has struck the last essay from the syllabus.
Sometimes it is lesson enough
to sit in the darkness with a movie, the familiar

hands of the clock jerking toward the bell.
One boy types *#timidlyinvincible*. Another
hurries through a worksheet for General Astronomy.

It is not too late to do the math, to triangulate stars,
to press a painted hand to the senior wall.
Outside a flatbed truck has backed up to the curb.

The driver unwinds a hose from the water tank
and begins to soak the newly planted shrubs,
the small potatoes, the upstarts.

Passing Period

Classes are changing, and although I made it to the door quickly, I am beaten by a teacher from across the hall. He pees slowly, washes his hands front and back, dries them carefully with too many paper towels. I hear him pumping them from the dispenser the way I used to jack-up my BB gun. Then there's another pause, one that I cannot account for. His hand should be turning the door handle, unlatching the dead bolt. My guess is that he combs his thick hair, checks his nostrils for hangers, tongues the gaps between his teeth. In a moment the bell will ring. My students will be in class, milling between their desks, shooting Instagrams into cyberspace. The vice principal walks the hall with his clipboard. As I turn the corner, he taps out a reprimand on his iPad.

old coach   dribbling the basketball through the gym's twilight

ABOUT THE RATTLE CHAPBOOK SERIES

The Rattle Chapbook Series publishes and distributes a chapbook to all of *Rattle*'s print subscribers along with each quarterly issue of the magazine. Most selections are made through the annual Rattle Chapbook Prize competition (deadline: January 15th). For more information, and to order other chapbooks from the series, visit our website.

www.Rattle.com/*chapbooks*